FOSAS

ON THE TRAIL

STUDYING
**SECRETIVE
ANIMALS**
IN THE WILD

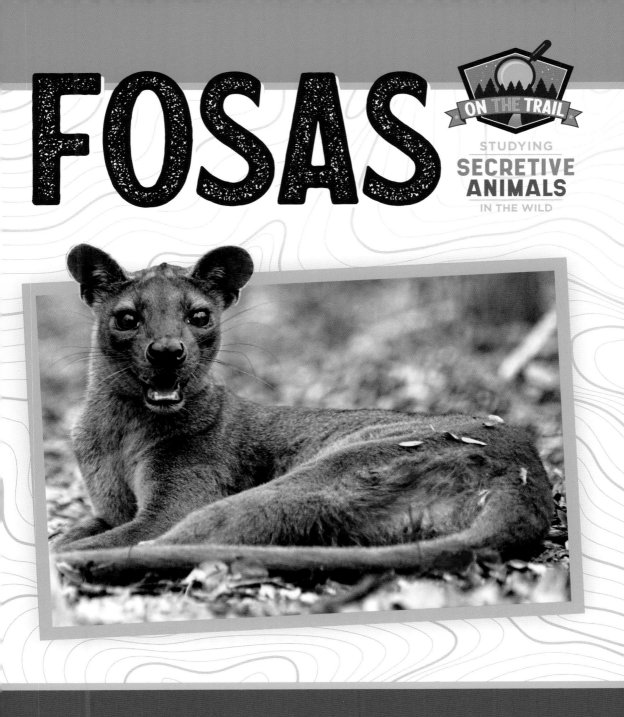

by Joyce Markovics

CHERRY LAKE PRESS

Published in the United States of America by Cherry Lake Publishing Group
Ann Arbor, Michigan
www.cherrylakepublishing.com

Reading Adviser: Marla Conn, MS Ed., Literacy specialist, Read-Ability, Inc.
Content Adviser: Katey Duffey
Book Designer: Ed Morgan

Photo Credits: © Angela N Perryman/Shutterstock, cover and title page; © freepik.com, TOC; © Dennis van de Water/Shutterstock, 4–5; © freepik.com, 4; © worldswildlifewonders/Shutterstock, 5; © Joel Quimby, 6; © Dirk M deBoer/Shutterstock, 7; © Zaruba Ondrej/Shutterstock, 8; © JAVIER CORDERO HUECAS/Shutterstock, 9; Wikimedia Commons, 9; © Dmitry Shkurin/Shutterstock, 10–11; © Hajakely/Shutterstock, 12; © Aldelo Piomica/Shutterstock, 13 top; © Danny Ye/Shutterstock, 13 bottom; © Poetic Penguin/Shutterstock, 14; © Miroslav Halama/Shutterstock, 15; © Vaclav Sebek/Shutterstock, 16; Wikimedia Commons, 17; © Joel Quimby, 18; © Darwin Mayhew/Evolving Light Photography, 19; © Dudarev Mikhail/Shutterstock, 20; © Karik/Shutterstock, 21; © takmat71/Shutterstock, 22; © Luke Dollar, 23; © Dietmar Temps/Shutterstock, 24; © MyImages-Micha/Shutterstock, 25; © Joel Quimby, 26; © Naples Zoo, 27; © Dudarev Mikhail/Shutterstock, 28; © RJ Endall/Shutterstock, 29; © Manekina Serafima/Shutterstock, 31.

Library of Congress Cataloging-in-Publication Data
Names: Markovics, Joyce L., author.
Title: Fosas / by Joyce L. Markovics.
Description: First edition. | Ann Arbor, Michigan : Cherry Lake Publishing, [2021] | Series: On the trail: studying secretive animals in the wild | Includes bibliographical references and index. | Audience: Ages 10 | Audience: Grades 4-6
Identifiers: LCCN 2020030347 (print) | LCCN 2020030348 (ebook) | ISBN 9781534180451 (hardcover) | ISBN 9781534182165 (paperback) | ISBN 9781534183179 (ebook) | ISBN 9781534181465 (pdf)
Subjects: LCSH: Fossa (Mammals)—Juvenile literature.
Classification: LCC QL737.C28 M37 2021 (print) | LCC QL737.C28 (ebook) | DDC 599.74/2—dc23
LC record available at https://lccn.loc.gov/2020030347
LC ebook record available at https://lccn.loc.gov/2020030348

Printed in the United States of America
Corporate Graphics

CONTENTS

TRAPPED!

Conservation biologist Luke Dollar held his finger up to his lips, signaling everyone on his team to be quiet. It was a May morning in a forest in Madagascar. Huge baobab (BEY-oh-bab) trees rose overhead like giant umbrellas. "You follow behind," whispered Luke. The team tiptoed, being careful not to make any loud noises. Up ahead was a wire cage about the size of a big suitcase. Huddled in the back of the cage was a long, brown animal with large, amber-colored eyes.

LOOK CLOSER

Madagascar is an island country off the coast of Africa. It's the fourth-largest island on Earth! Fosas live only in Madagascar. They're one of the largest native carnivores found there.

The silence was broken by a deep growl and snort coming from within the cage. Then, suddenly, there was a burst of movement. The catlike animal arched its back and thrashed around the cage, trying to escape. Luke had captured a fosa (FOO-sah), one of the most secretive and deadly **predators** in the world.

Although they look like small panthers, fosas are members of their own family of carnivores.

WILD
WHODUNIT

Luke's first introduction to fosas was in 1994. At the time, he was tracking lemurs in Madagascar with a local guide. One day, he picked up a strange signal. It came from a tracking collar worn by a lemur named Stanzi. But Luke knew the battery in Stanzi's collar had stopped working years ago. He was puzzled.

Conservation biologist Luke Dollar holding a fosa

LOOK **CLOSER**

Lemurs are a kind of tree-dwelling primate. They often have pointed snouts and long tails.

Luke traced the signal to an area in the forest. There, he found clumps of lemur fur, bones, and the broken collar on the ground. Nearby, was a fresh pile of droppings. After some **detective** work, Luke figured out what had happened. "The predator that attacked the animal had clamped down so hard on the collar that it reconnected the battery wires, which had broken long ago," said Luke. His guide gasped, "A fosa got it!"

CRYPTIC CREATURES

In Madagascar, local people tell stories of fosas stealing babies from cribs and **butchering** flocks of chickens. "Be good, or the fosa will get you!" they warn their children. All these stories made Luke even more curious about the mysterious animal.

Another tall tale tells of fosas licking sleeping people, putting them under a spell, and then eating them!

So Luke decided to **devote** his life to learning about an animal he had never even seen. He went back to the United States to research the fosa. Luke learned that a few U.S. zoos had fosas, but very little was actually known about wild fosa behavior. "Here was a mysterious predator which sat atop the **food chain** . . . yet no one knew anything about it," says Luke. He returned to Madagascar to uncover everything he possibly could about the fosa.

LOOK CLOSER

Today, there are around 50 fosas living in zoos in the United States.

SLEEK AND POWERFUL

When Luke finally saw his first fosa in the wild, he was amazed. "Your first thought is that it's a cat," he says. "It looks sort of like a cougar or mountain lion but on a smaller scale."

A fosa's tail is about as long as its body.

An adult fosa is about 6 feet (2 meters) long from the tip of its nose to the end of its tail. At 30 pounds (14 kilograms), it weighs less than an average dog. The animal is long, lean, and very muscular. "It has claws like a cat," says Luke. But its big toe is on the outside of its foot so that it can grip and climb trees.

A fosa has large, powerful jaws and teeth. All of these traits make the animal a ferocious predator. "It is king of the jungle," says Luke.

LOOK CLOSER

The fosa's ancient relative, *Cryptoprocta spelea*, weighed around 45 pounds (20 kg). It might have hunted huge lemurs that no longer exist.

FOREST HOME

Madagascar's forests are home to many **unique** animals. Eighty percent of these creatures are found nowhere else in the world! Lemurs, for example, live only in Madagascar. There are more than 100 **species** of lemur, ranging in size from tiny mouse lemurs to 20-pound (9 kg) indri lemurs.

Mouse lemurs are the smallest primates in the world. Each one weighs only about as much as a slice of bread!

There's only one island predator that can take down a large lemur—the fosa. For protection, lemurs sleep in groups in trees. But fosas are expert climbers. Luke has discovered that they **ambush** lemurs in trees. Fosas' long tails help them balance as they leap from branch to branch. Luke often finds the remains of lemurs attacked by fosas near trees where lemurs sleep.

A sleeping ring-tailed lemur

Fosas can crawl up and down trees like squirrels.

LOOK **CLOSER**

Fosas chirp, purr, and even yelp. Each sound has a different meaning.

FIERCE FOSAS

Luke calls fosas "killing machines." When they attack, "the fosa is capable of **explosive** speed," he explains. *Wham!* A fosa rushes in and strikes with a bite to its victim's head. According to Luke, a fosa can crush its prey's skull in one chomp. Then it uses its front claws to rip open the animal's belly.

A fosa looking for prey in the water

"There is absolutely no nervousness," says scientist Clare Hawkins, who also studied fosas in Madagascar. "They just get on about their business." She believes the fosa hunts like a cat. And like a cat, Luke adds, a fosa "will eat anything with a heartbeat." After **devouring** a big, bloody meal, fosas lick their fur to keep clean, just like cats.

LOOK CLOSER

In addition to lemurs, fosas feed on rodents, reptiles, birds, and even fish.

TRACKING

Finding fosas to study in the wild is no easy task. "They are just so elusive," says Luke. "They don't want to be seen." Sometimes, it can take days or weeks to find one.

A fosa high up in a tree

LOOK CLOSER

Fosas have scent glands near their tail and chest. The glands give off a powerful odor that smells a little like rotten meat. The animals rub the glands on rocks and trees to communicate with other fosas.

In April 2000, Luke and his team spent a week looking for fosas, but failed to spot a single one. Late one night, Luke set up several wire cage traps. Each one held stinky meat, one of the fosa's favorite snacks. The next day, Luke discovered that the meat was gone. The trap had been ripped from its place and rolled more than 10 feet (3 meters)! In the distance, Luke saw the long, low shadow of what looked like a fosa. It stopped briefly, then vanished like a ghost.

Luke often struggles to find and catch fosas to study.

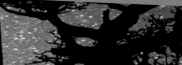

CATCH AND RELEASE

Trapping fosas in the wild requires creativity and patience. Over time, Luke has trapped more than 100 fosas. When he catches one, he gives it a drug to make it sleepy. After that, he and his team measure every part of the animal, including its snout, legs, and teeth. He also collects blood and **tissue** samples. This helps Luke learn about the overall health of the animal.

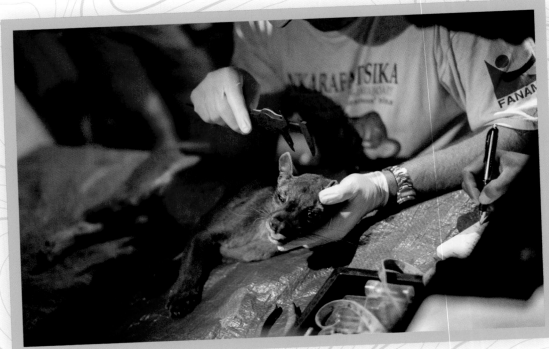

Luke measuring a fosa's head

Luke works with a team of people, including veterinarians and other researchers. Together, they gather and share information about fosas.

Often, Luke and his team put special GPS (Global Positioning System) collars on the captured animals. The collars allow him to track the movements of the animal in the thick forests. After the collar is secured and switched on, the animal wakes up and is released back in the forest.

A collared fosa

AT RISK

Forests covered much of Madagascar when people first arrived on the island thousands of years ago. Today, most of the island's trees have been cleared to make room for farmland. Less than 10 percent of the original forest remains. "The vast majority of the country is totally deforested," according to Luke. There is little suitable **habitat** left for fosas, their prey, and Madagascar's other incredible animals.

Many forests in Madagascar are burned down by local people.

As a result of habitat destruction, many of Madagascar's plants and animals have become **extinct**. And those that remain are under serious threat, including the fierce fosa. "As soon as there's any habitat disturbance, fosa numbers fall," says Luke. He guesses that only about 3,000 fosas are left on the island.

This rare blue-eyed lemur is in danger of dying out.

LOOK **CLOSER**

During the past 1,500 years, 17 species of lemur have become extinct. All lemur species are currently in danger of dying out.

"SAVE THE FOSA"

As fosa habitat shrinks, the animals leave the forests in search of food. This puts them in great danger. Many fosas enter villages where they prey on chickens. This angers the villagers, who, in turn, attack and kill the fosas. Some people on the island also hunt fosas for food or use their body parts for **traditional** medicine.

A fosa sniffing dishes in an outdoor kitchen

Luke is fighting to stop the killing of fosas and to educate the people of Madagascar about how important the animals really are. He passes out posters that say, "Save the Fosa. Save the Harvest." Luke explains that rats and pigs often destroy crops before farmers can harvest them. Fosas prey on these pests and therefore can help save the crops. After people make that connection, they discover "a newfound appreciation for the fosa," says Luke.

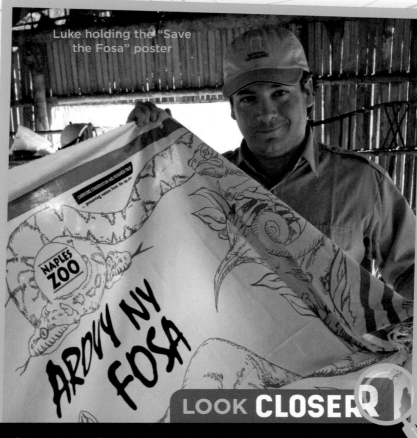

Luke holding the "Save the Fosa" poster

NAPLES ZOO

AROVY NY FOSA

LOOK **CLOSER**

The "Save the Fosa. Save the Harvest" poster is written in Malagasy, the language of Madagascar.

OUTREACH

Luke saw firsthand how education is the key to changing people's **perception** of fosas. So he started a **scholarship** program for local children who live near fosa habitats. Children who participate in the program agree to protect the wildlife of Madagascar once they complete their schooling.

Some of the children in the scholarship program become forest rangers. "Education is the single most important tool for improving conservation in Madagascar," Luke says.

Luke also helps raise awareness about fosas by taking young scientists on nature hikes in Madagascar. On one such hike, he came upon a small village with women singing folk songs. Luke was so impressed, he asked the women if he could pay them to sing for **ecotourists**. They agreed. At the time, the villagers were cutting down the forest in order to farm and earn money. The women now had a new way of making a living—and the forest could be saved.

LOOK **CLOSER**

Luke has worked with Friends of Madagascar, a group that has built and rebuilt 40 schools in Madagascar. This has helped thousands of schoolchildren.

THE FUTURE

In order to save the fosa, Luke knows he must help local people survive. "When they can earn way more walking a group of tourists through the forest than they can by cutting it down," he says, "they become far more interested in protecting what's there." Luke also sees the importance of investing in Madagascar's future leaders through his scholarship programs and building schools.

Luke usually travels to Madagascar three times per year.

"No matter how fierce the fosa is, it still needs a home to survive," says Luke. "I wake up every morning knowing I'm one of the luckiest guys on Earth, because I'm doing exactly what I want to do and it's going to make a difference."

LOOK **CLOSER**

The Naples Zoo in Florida has a special fosa exhibit and supports Luke's work in Madagascar.

Luke speaking with schoolchildren about fosas at the Naples Zoo

FAST FACTS

FOSAS

Scientific Name
Cryptoprocta ferox

Physical Description
Reddish-brown fur with a lighter colored belly

Size
Up to 6 feet (2 m) long, including the tail

Weight
Up to 30 pounds (14 kg)

Main Diet
Lemurs, rodents, birds, reptiles, and other small animals

Habitat
Madagascar

Life Span
Up to 20 years

DID YOU KNOW?

- A fosa can draw its claws back into its paws like a cat.

- Fosas release a stinky smell from their scent glands when they're frightened.

- Fosas travel up to 16 miles (26 kilometers) a day to find food.

- Fosa mothers give birth to between two and six cubs. The cubs are born without teeth and with their eyes closed.

GLOSSARY

ambush (AM-bush) to attack someone from a hiding place

butchering (BUCH-ur-ing) brutally killing

carnivores (KAHR-nuh-vorz) meat-eating animals

conservation biologist (kahn-sur-VAY-shuhn bye-AH-luh-jist) a scientist who studies how best to protect wildlife and natural resources

detective (dih-TEK-tiv) concerning a crime and its investigation

devote (dih-VOHT) to give your time, effort, or attention to some purpose

devouring (dih-VOUR-ing) eating hungrily and quickly

ecotourists (EE-koh-toor-ists) people who travel to natural environments to see wildlife and support conservation efforts

elusive (ih-LOO-siv) very hard to catch or find

explosive (ik-SPLOH-siv) related to a sudden increase in something, such as speed

extinct (ik-STINGKT) no longer found alive

food chain (FOOD CHAYN) an ordered arrangement of animals and plants in which each feeds on the one below it in the chain

habitat (HAB-ih-tat) the natural home of an animal or a plant

native (NAY-tiv) an animal belonging to a particular place

perception (pur-SEP-shuhn) how a person sees and understands something

predators (PRED-uh-turz) animals that hunt and kill other animals for food

primate (PRYE-mate) any member of the group of mammals that includes monkeys, apes, and humans

scent glands (SENT GLANDZ) body parts that give off a liquid with a strong smell

scholarship (SKAH-lur-ship) money given to a person to attend school

species (SPEE-sheez) a group of similar animals that can reproduce with each other

tissue (TISH-oo) a mass of similar cells that form a particular part of the body

traditional (truh-DISH-uh-nuhl) relating to a long-established way of thinking

unique (yoo-NEEK) one of a kind; like no other

vanished (VAN-ishd) disappeared from sight

READ MORE

Goldish, Meish. *Fossa: A Fearsome Predator*. New York: Bearport Publishing, 2008.

Oluonye, Mary N. *Madagascar*. Minneapolis: Lerner Publications, 2010

Solway, Andrew. *Killer Carnivores*. Chicago: Heinemann Library, 2005.

LEARN MORE ONLINE

Happy Hollow Park and Zoo: Fosa
http://happyhollow.org/explore/zoo/zoo-in-the-hollow/fossa-2

Naples Zoo: Fosa
https://www.napleszoo.org/fosa

National Geographic Learning: An Interview with Dr. Luke Dollar—Conservationist/National Geographic Explorer
https://www.youtube.com/watch?v=vMAV5tv6pgY

San Diego Zoo: Meet the Mysterious Fosa
https://zoonooz.sandiegozoo.org/zoonooz/meet-the-mysterious-fossa

Zoo Atlanta: Fosas
https://zooatlanta.org/animal/fossa

INDEX

ABOUT THE AUTHOR

Joyce Markovics has authored more than 150 books for young readers. She's wild about rare and unusual animals and is passionate about preservation. Joyce lives in an old house along the Hudson River in Ossining, New York. She would like to thank Luke Dollar for his generous contribution to this book and to the wildlife of Madagascar.